WALK WITH ME
INTO THE LIGHT

EILEEN CURTEIS

CCB Publishing
British Columbia, Canada

Walk With Me Into the Light

Copyright ©2022 by Eileen Curteis
ISBN-13   978-1-77143-547-5
First Edition

Library and Archives Canada Cataloguing in Publication
Curteis, Eileen, 1942-, author
Walk with me into the light / written and illustrated by Eileen Curteis. -- First edition.
Issued in print and electronic formats.
ISBN 978-1-77143-547-5 (softcover).--ISBN 978-1-77143-548-2 (PDF)
Additional cataloguing data available from Library and Archives Canada

Cover artwork and interior drawings, as well as all poems, are by Eileen Curteis.

Cover design by Carey Pallister.

Author photo credit: Carey Pallister

Publisher: CCB Publishing
               British Columbia, Canada
               www.ccbpublishing.com

Just as a city seated
on a mountaintop cannot be hid,
so too must we let our light shine.
Matthew 5:14

To Claire

Written for my friends
who travel the journey with me.

Eileen Curteis, usa

Acknowledgements

Carey Pallister, for her loving support, digital skills and artistic arrangement of my book. Susan McCaslin for her friendship and periodic editing skills. Lynn Harvey for her Foreword and for her affirming ways. Jason Curteis for his astute and touching Preface. Thanks also to my wonderful friends who have generously acknowledged my work on the back cover of my book. Paul Rabinovitch, for his expertise and compatibility in publishing a number of my books, including this one.

CONTENTS

Photo of our Blessed Foundress with the ball of light: Ana Martinez

Photo taken from the e-book version of *Witness for Our Time*

Dedicated to Blessed Marie Anne Blondin
(1809-1890)
Foundress of the Sisters of Saint Anne
September 8, 1850

ESTHER BLONDIN
HIDDEN SAINT FOR OUR TIME

Mother Marie Anne
Foundress of the Sisters of Saint Anne
the unwanted part of you
is what I feel drawn into.

Yourself
discarded like a scrap of paper
I feel you know me
because of that.

When I'm downcast
it's the genealogy
of your soul
I climb into.

Like a modern-day Mary
you brought the God of love to us
no hierarchy in it
just love.

You were an ordinary soul
nothing of pomp
or the elite in you.

And, yet,
anyone touching
the hem of your garment
would have known
what holy is.

FOREWORD – LYNN HARVEY

Life is a process of becoming, the emergence from the darkness and physical density of our living reality to the true light of our being. Sister Eileen Curteis' book of art and poetry, *Walk With Me into the Light,* captures this message beautifully. Her inspiring work opens the heart, mind and soul in a way that evokes the very core of our purpose of being. Each verse of her remarkable poetry vibrates with vitality and brings home to us the truth of how we long to live our lives more gloriously.

The message relayed through Sister Eileen to us is embedded with hope and offers the reader assurance and confirmation that this transition is possible. As a reader of her work, I am struck by the simplicity and exquisite delivery of the flow of words contained within this thought-provoking volume, bringing forth a book of pure treasures that many will easily relate to.

Like the metamorphosis of the often-described ugly caterpillar that emerges like a glorious winged creature, I am reminded of a quote from Anais Nin that aptly captures the essence of these divinely guided poems: "And the day came when the risk to remain tight in a bud was more painful than the risk it took to blossom."

Without a doubt, Sister Eileen has tapped into the

very source of our being, bringing forth the Love, Compassion, Wisdom and Guidance inherent in us all!

PREFACE – JASON CURTEIS

When you leave Eileen Curteis alone with her God, amazing things happen. Words, ideas and understanding start to flow, as she chases her truth down, using metaphor and rhythm. The resulting poems and sketches, inspired during the Covid-19 pandemic, speak of a journey towards healing and finally arriving at one's authentic self.

I'm proud to say that I have played a small part in that journey. When I was eighteen years old, I opened myself to the universe, asking to be a conduit for celebrating my cherished Aunt, on the occasion of her 25th anniversary of entering religious life. This is the poem that came almost immediately:

LIGHT OF THE NEW DAWN

A harsh word you would not say
about the most insignificant of creatures.
In your quiet loudness you powerfully voice
the beauty and goodness in all things.
And even when your lips fall silent,
your heart still sings of hope and love
for everything.
One can see it in your eyes, ever smiling.
Your youthful spirit has not been killed
by the cruel world outside,
for it does not exist, at least in your eyes.
You make everyone's dreams your own,

because you have room for them all
in your heart.
Your friends are limitless,
everyone is your friend.
Your enemies uncountable,
for there are none to count.
To the world you give many things,
but more than the light of the new dawn
which has begun to shine
or the first sounds of a child,
you bring hope.
And there is nothing
more important than that.
Nothing.

When I wrote that poem, I felt like I had channeled the truth, and for me, I had. What I didn't know was that it would be a signpost and a beacon throughout my Aunt's life. For her, not a place she had arrived at, but a place she was striving towards. My truth was her promise to the future.

Happily, that future has arrived, and with it these poems and sketches.

INTRODUCTION – EILEEN CURTEIS

Sometimes the Spirit of God sweeps down upon a person and takes you by surprise. Such was my encounter on Saturday, May 2nd, 2020, the second day of my annual Sister of Saint Ann retreat. It was 3:00 am in the morning when I was suddenly awakened from sleep with the words: "It is never too late to open your throat and let the songbirds in." At that moment I knew the poet in me was being invited to speak again. Quickly, I hopped out of bed and wrote the words down.

For the next seventy nights, I continued to be awakened with words that were given to me in seed form and that would develop into a poem the following day. I would then feel the poem inside me and a black and white sketch would emerge depicting the message that was in the poem.

On the seventieth day, when I was awakened in the wee hours of the morning, I sensed that the poem that was being given would be the last one for the book. I had no idea how the poem would emerge but when it did, I knew the significance of it. I titled the poem, Birthing of a White Owl, and it reminded me of an actual experience that had occurred 25 years prior at Queenswood, our Sister of Saint Ann retreat and spirituality centre in Victoria, BC.

Recounting the story now, I remember it was an unusually dark night around 8:00 pm when I entered the Queenswood driveway. Coming toward the windshield of my car, I saw a large white ball and immediately put my foot on the brake. It was the face of a white fluffy owl that looked straight into my eyes and then flew up into a cedar tree. At that precise moment, I remember feeling the inner assurance from a Higher Realm that the new path of my Christ-centered Reiki healing ministry was indeed the right one for me.

Actually, my whole life has been guided by this transcendent Love Force. Most probably this explains once again how these poems during this pandemic time have been given to me as gift, not just for my own healing but for others who travel a similar path as mine.

AWAKENING

Like an alarm clock
blaring in the night
wake up and know:
It is I who am coming!

Flowing out of my pen
is the unseen
unheard of ink
I am writing into you now.

It's the script
you've been waiting for
so cast your nose upward
and smell the clean air
coming into you.

Lifting the veil
from your closed eyes
open your blocked ears
and hear again
the orchestra of sound.

I am the untouchable Mystery
living nowhere and everywhere
at the same time.

Try touching
my hidden face
and you will find it rampant
with glee.

EVOLUTIONARY MOTHER

Coming out of a world
closed in on itself
we are the new species
the crushed-out ones
staggering to live.

It may be true
you've given us
the legs of a giant
but still
we are your children
no bigger
than a grain of sand
washed over
by the waves of the sea.

In You
we are nothing
and everything
at the same time.
The whole beach is ours
the soft sand
on which you planted us
so we could grow
into the yet more
of You.

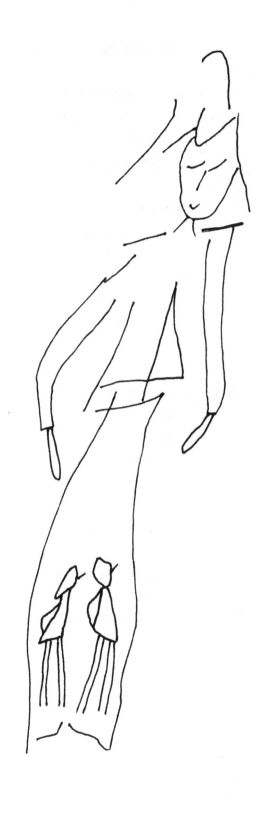

FULLY ALIVE

Barefoot and naked
in your mother's womb:
I am the river of life
that began you.

Untarnished at birth
but blackened now
you dislike the place
you have slid into
the dark hole
that turns
the skin of your soul murky.

You could live in clean water,
you know,
if you stopped
your loitering.

Flying above the earth
as you tried to do
is an illusion.
You must sink deep down
into it
with your backpack
full of nothing.

Then
you shall grow
into the One who began you.

STILLNESS WITHIN

It's never too late
to open your throat
and let
the songbirds in.

They have known
devastation
before you.
Their clipped wings
have fallen prey
to the earth.

Their song silenced
by the tumult
of the wind
and in their drudgery
they have flown
higher than you.

Go there.
Be there.

In the current
of a new wind
you will find
as in a whisper
the harmony
you long for.

RISEN ONES

Tangled
in my own anatomy
I'm shedding
the false skin
of my old self.

Forged
in love
I'm leaving behind
the crumpled-up face
of a bitter woman.

Discarding
once and for all
the tomb
in which I lived
I'm rising
as the risen one.

Assemblies
of people
are out there
rising with me.

Nothing
can stop the Force
with which we travel!

SOLIDITY OF OUR GLOBAL HOME

In a moment of terror
you dislodged us
from our homes.

Unlocking
the door of our hearts
you came
like a broom in the night
and the dust
came swishing out of us.

We fell down
and you shook
our rafters clean.

Feeling our fragility
was like jumping
into a garbage can
you can't get out of.

And, yet,
you picked us up
like a piece of splintered wood
and made the perishable ones
imperishable.

And to our creaky home
our global home
you said:
There will be no more teetering.

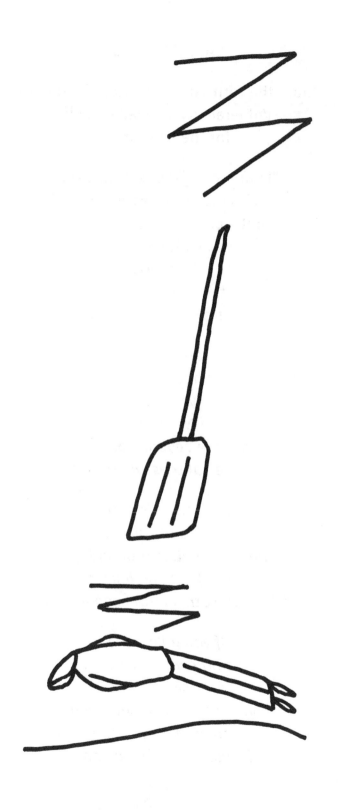

VAST GALAXIES

Under the torn skin of the ripped off mask
Vulnerability showed herself
for the first time.

"I am the frigid one," she said.
"As much as I want love
not a cold bone in my body
will let it come in.
I love God
but a steep wall
has grown between us."

Yes, came the Voice.
I am not the barrier
you are.
I want you
to move beyond yourself
into the galaxies where I am.

The gateway is narrow
and people
put parameters around Me,
high walls and fences
to exclude others from coming in.

If you follow Me
the gateway will open.
I am Love incarnate
and nothing can deter you
from getting to know
the vastness of who I am.

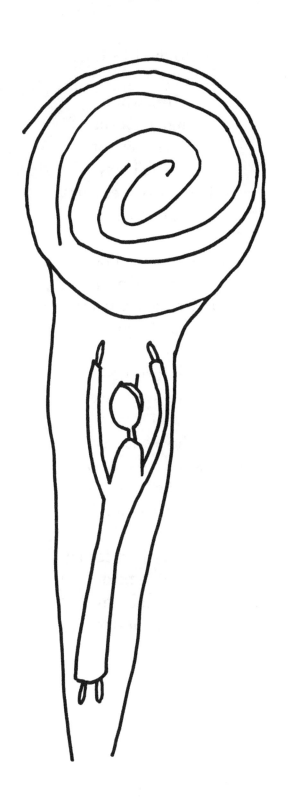

FLOURISHING TIME

Pure white
and innocent
as a snowdrop
she fell prey
to her worst enemy
ignorance.

Squashed down
stepped over
the ground grew fertile
under her.

Intoxicated
by the sweet scent
of lilac
she wondered
when it would be
her time
to bloom.

In the farthest corner
of the field
small daisies
were turning
their faces
to the sun.

Yearning
to be one of them
she remained
in her small plot of land
with the riddle
of new growth
ripening in her.

Shying away
from making herself
known
she knew
that in this garden
no one
is anonymous.

POLISHED WISDOM

Wisdom
is knowledgeable
not in the way
you would think her
to be.

She travels quietly
on nimble feet
disturbing no one.

One look at her
and an empty cup
becomes full.

Anything forlorn
jagged
or rough
she sits with it
in thorny places.

And to the wilted flower
on the stem
she brings back
new life.

Even on dark days
when everything else
fails
She makes the gold
glitter.

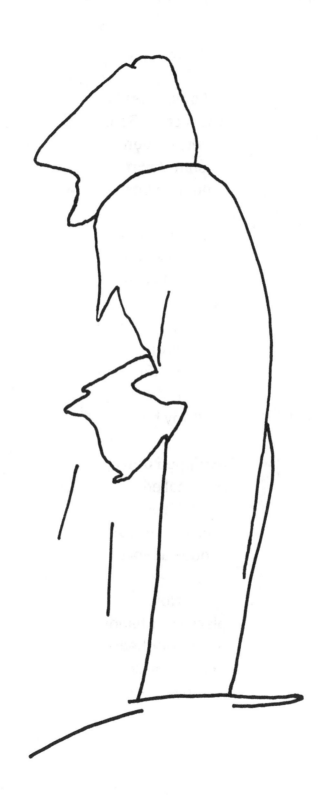

FREEDOM

Sometimes
the face of God
gets hidden
shut down
put in a box.

If you've known
the sterility
of life this way
say to yourself:
It's not God's hand
sucking
the life
out of me
it's my hand.

Stripped down
naked
bare
that's what truth
does to you.

Now
place your hands
over your heart
and let the scabs
fly free.

CHRIST LOVE RETURNING

Hidden
in the hollow stump of a tree
some say:
Christ is not alive today
but I know He is!

Look around you and see:
red blood, my blood, your blood
everybody's blood.

Disastrous as it is
you cannot put a stop to war
without a phoenix rising in you.

Idealistic as it may seem
there's something soft
in harsh.

Something noble
so noble
that nothing
not even a missile
can destroy
the Life Force in you.

What is certain
we will all one day die
and if you haven't met
the beauty
of the Son of God beforehand
you will meet Him now.

SAILING FREE

In my past life
which was yesterday
I could not howl loud enough
to be heard.

Ancestral faces
were pulling me backwards
when I wanted
to move forward.

Today
with the chiming
of a clock at night
I know
Someone vaster
than I am
has entered me.

Travelling beside her
in deeper waters
I'm no longer
mooring my boat
on the shore.

Even
in the roughest waters
if you put a lid on my tongue
I will speak
God's name.

SUN DAUGHTER

Falling in love
with Love
nothing could hold her down
not even a dark cloud
casting its shadow over her.

She was a pure soul
innocent and naive
with joy
bubbling up
like a fountain.

Forgetting to ground herself
she was up there
soaring with the eagles
when suddenly
the winds shifted
and the rains
came pelting down.

Shattered as she was
nothing
could pound the goodness
out of her.

Nothing
not even a holocaust
could stop the sun
from shining through.

BIRD IN FLIGHT

Too many bars
restraining her wings
the caged in bird
knew early
how not to fly.

Locked
into a life
that was not good for her
she could whimper
all day long
and still not be heard.

One day
with wisdom in her beak
she was found
pushing back
the bars of her cage.

Nothing
could stop her now
not even a room with walls in it.

Flying high
we heard her singing:
"When the grouchy part of me
gets smoothed out
I'll be humming
a new tune for you."

GLOBAL LIGHT

Clay feet
stumbling over
a torn down fence
this is not the end of you
just the beginning.

Be dry, be thirsty
be hungry
then you will know
I come to you
as water
to clean out the gutters
after the garbage is gone.

I am the Alpha
and the Omega
the beginning
and the end.

Nothing dies in Me
not even the last ash
of the burnt-out fire in you.

Written
or unwritten
I am the Author of all life
so pick up your global pen
and let the signature
of my Light
implant itself within you.

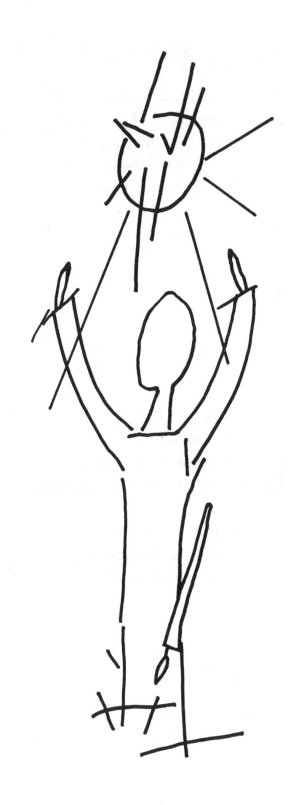

SELF LOVE

Sitting quietly
on the porch of her being
a rickety old woman
grew to loving
the small girl within her.

"I am older than you are,"
she said,
"much older
and, yet,
it seems like yesterday
you were bursting
the buttons open on my coat.

Like a disturbed child
or a lone seagull crying in the wind
you wanted my attention
but I couldn't give it to you, then.

Tugging at my scarf for warmth
even that left you cold
on the inside.

Today
I am turning
the book of my life
inside-out
and loving you
the way I should."

GOD WHISTLES

Once
the whistle of Love
gets blown into you
you cannot stop
her coming.

Try shoving her
out of your life
and she'll go on
being the ballerina
dancing in you.

Put a barrier
or tall fence up
and she'll knock
the barricade down.

Sit in aridity
and she'll go on
standing
in the lake of your soul.

She comes
not to punish you
but to tell you
her name is God
so don't put
a label on her.

SPIRIT LOVE

Even though
life can be
a tripping up game
put a kite
under your limp arms
and let your feet fly free.

Let go, let loose
let the stale air
blow through you.

When Spirit comes
be ready for anything
even the plopping
of bird poop on you
can bring merriment
to your soul!

She loves humour
so squeeze your nose shut
and show her
the dog shit on your shoe.

She's with you always
and whether it's the sour
or sweet side of your face
you wake up with,
Spirit will go on loving you
just the way you are.

EARTH DANCER

Earth
is the dance floor of God
luxuriate
and rejoice in it.

Broaden your vision
untie the tangled knot
on your shoe
swirl your skirt
clockwise.

Going around
squinting at life
is a ridiculous pattern
you've fallen into.

Soften up some more
travel with new slippers
where one foot
flows into the other.

Prance
across the room
out the door
and into the world
that awaits you.

Like fresh water
flowing from a stream
guzzle it in now.

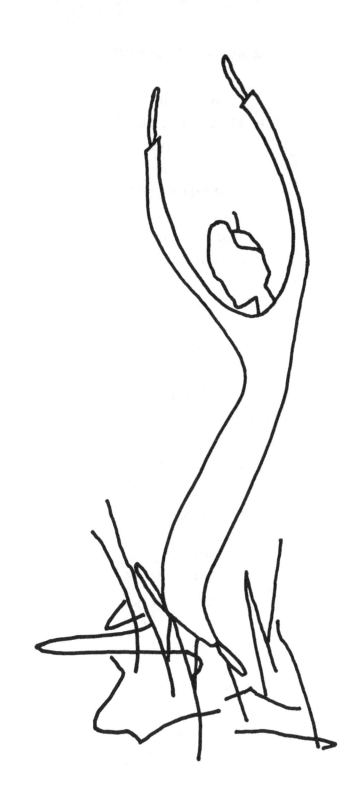

ROADWAY LEARNING

A lifetime
of being used to a small God
I grew weary of it.

Too many rules
in the old way
pushed me
into something new.

Seeing
what expansion looks like
I sometimes think
the new God
sitting in my car
is evolving faster than I am.

Out on the highway
she spurts ahead
when I lag behind.

Encouraging me
to put my foot
on the gas pedal
she takes me
where I need to go.

It's a big God
in front of the wheel
and not a small one
I choose to follow.

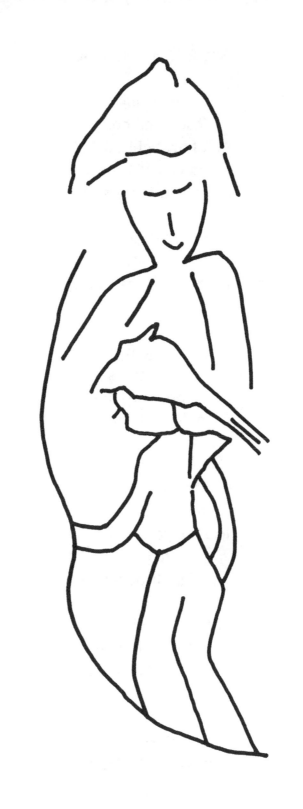

SKY-ROCKETING GOD

Try living
inside the body
of my tight skin
and you will know
what held-in feels like.

Harming no one
but myself
I play the game called
"pretend".

Shielding myself
from others
no one sees me
only God does.

Aching
to be known
I need something
like the gong of a bell
to go
rippling through me.

I need an alive God
who rings into me
the chime of a new day.

A God
with whom
I can go sky-rocketing.

EXOTIC ROSE

Free limbs
dancing the storm out of me
that's how I got to know You.

"Follow
the stream of your soul,"
You said,
"and it will lead you
where you need to go.

Not everything
will be palatable
but see, touch, feel, smell
and taste it anyway
even sour cherries
have a sweetness in them.

When you sprout your own wings
not everyone
will welcome the way you fly
but fly anyway.

Be exotic
like the rose
and say to her:
'The thorns
that made me bleed
brought me home
to my true self.'"

BEST MUSIC SCRIPT

Wired differently
whoever composes my music
knows what she's doing.

With an element of surprise in it
I could be a tap dancer
on a waltzing floor.
Following after me
could be a jazz band
ecstatic with sound
when I want
something ethereal.

Sitting in the symphony
I could be
smacking a buzzing bee
and still not be content
with my surroundings.

And then
there's the foolish part of me
wanting to be world famous.

Whether it be harmony
or disharmony I'm after,
the truth of the matter is this:
I guess I'm on a zigzag way
of walking a straight road
when there's a bit
of the crooked in me.

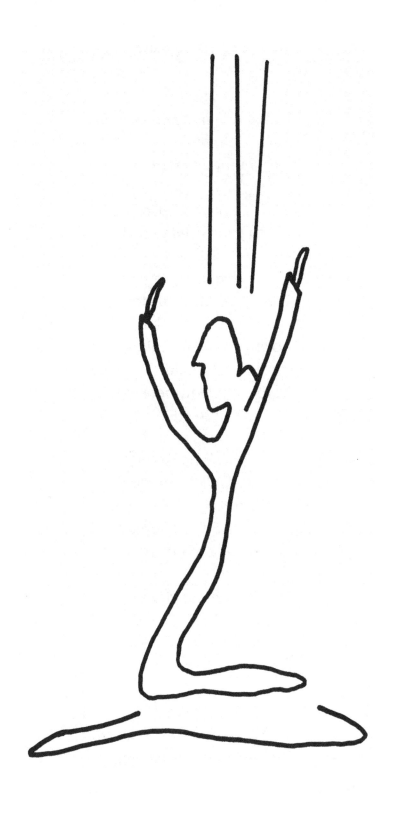

FACE OF INFINITY

Infinity
came rolling down the hill
and I
bumped into her.

Say good-bye
to your stunted self,
she said,
and marry me
not tomorrow but today.

Looking into my strained face
she said:
Let me blow new life
into you.

Let go of your wrinkles
and glide through
the tunnel of my arms
where I will pump
new air into you.

There's no charge
for my kind of Energy
it's free and open
and worth indulging in.

Travel with me
and the sun and the moon
and the stars will be yours.

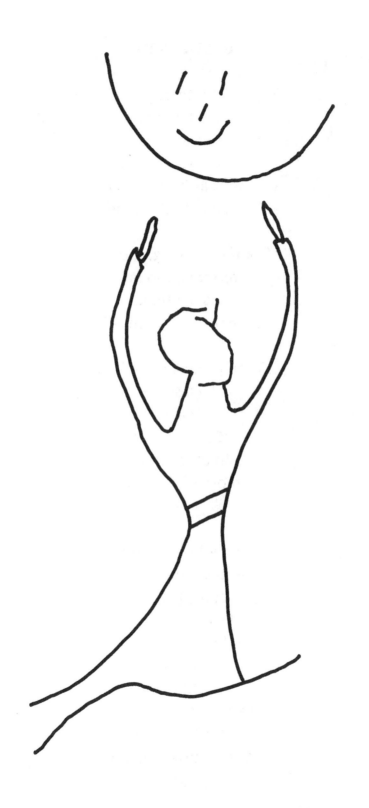

GREEN EARTH

Yesterday
when I was told
to clean up
my own back yard
the cells in my body
screeched otherwise.

"I am too young, too old
too thin, too fat
too anything
to make a difference."

Then picking myself up
like a spade
I said:
"Cut me open
and there will be
no more of the 'grizzly'
in me.

And when it comes
to the weedy part
of my garden
I shall sit softly
in the manure of it.

Others
shall sit there with me
and together
we shall grow it green."

RADIANT FINGERS

Falling in love
and out of it
you can't always
wend your way back in.

That's when you say:
"Like a hot flame
burning in me
I can tell you
what cold turned inward
feels like."

As much as you want love,
in the world of energy
nothing is permanent
only God is.

Now clutching your cold fingers
feel the trickle
of something warm
and radiant.

Then say to yourself:
"If this be God,
then let me indulge in it."

Momentary as it is
it's the luxury of immanence
you will go on
remembering.

INNOCENT CHILDREN

Like a sweet peach ready to be eaten
we come into our world
fresh and ripe for it with a story to tell.

Innocent children we are
splashing paint on the floor
giggling with glee
until we get reprimanded.

Off to school we go
tripping and falling into a classroom
where only the intelligent survive.

Chained down in a desk
our energy
wants to go
running down a hill.

Home at last
with mud on our cheeks
we wash ourselves quickly
so as not to be seen.

Innocent and good
bad and naughty
we sit at the dinner table
and learn:
Life is the playground
where intelligence begins
and school is only part of it.

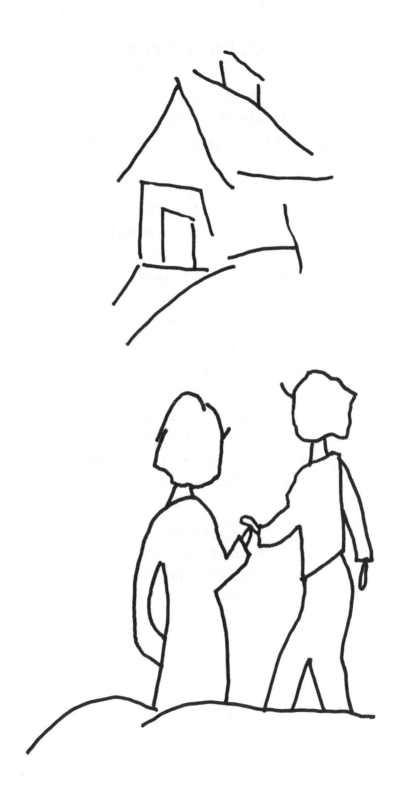

KNOWING WOMAN

Slivers gone now
I wake up thanking you
for your brutal punch upon my face.

Drinking your curdled milk
had turned me sour
and a phony lullaby at night
had pushed me
out of the bed beside you.

Sitting at a clean table now
I pop open the boil that burnt me
and the pus comes pouring out.

Like a church steeple
in a nearby town
I can hear the soft ringing of a bell
calling me home to my true self.

Flaring up
like a flame within me
my heart widens
and I feel the warmth of her
moving in me now.

My feet are steady
solid
as the rock of the ground
I stand on.

REBORN

You must not let
the crying world
explode over you.

Attend to home matters first
and say
to your stunted self:
When the volcano erupts
new growth is on its way.

Even the ash in your mouth
will taste different
so enjoy the flavour of it
while you can.

Unravel yourself
and the world
will unravel with you.

New sprouts will grow up
in the debris
and we will all
be better for it.

So put your paper dolly
to bed now
and let the real you
walk out of your house
clean, tall
and beautiful.

RAINBOW LIVING

Soft heart
iron strong
you can't go on
hiding your shrouded tears.

Protecting yourself
or peeking through
a black cloud
won't do it.

What you need
is torrential rain
and a flattened umbrella
placed under you.

Gasping for breath
you will come out
wearing binoculars
that let you see.

Radical sky
indigo-blue
purple-pink:
You'll be sitting
on a rainbow
flirting with the wind.

The old you
will have eroded
into something new.

HEALED WOUND

Falling prey to a numb wind
I felt something hard
like stone
gripping me.

Holding
my empty cup upward
I knew
I was a waterspout gone dry.

Inside my rusty heart
someone
had put a nail into it.

Lashing out
at no one but myself
self-pity
became the false god
sitting on my wounded knee.

Then
came Love
a truckload of it
nursing my wound better.

Inside
my rejoicing heart
nothing
not even the stab of a knife
can harm me now.

EVOLVING WORLD

Portrait of a blind woman
wanting to see
could be anyone of us.

Wanting to advance
but stumbling along,
the white cane we carry
is the crutch we lean on.

Standing dismally
on a bruised world
what we need now
are ethereal melodies
unseen, unheard of sounds
coming through
a violin, a flute, a trumpet.

A white lily
a red rose
a pink sky
anything that will uplift us
on the inside.

At the end of day
even if the earth
falls down dead
the clean finger of God
will evolve her
into something new!

KITE
SAILING IN THE WIND

Whatever is belligerent
nasty, hurtful
come out of that whirlwind now
and let my Energy
flow freely through you.

Sweet, innocent
lovely, pure
let go of the false image
of your former self.

Put on street clothes
get in touch
with the deep, the dark
and the ugly.

If nothing else
will heal you
let the warmth of my scarf
around you
bolster you up.

Above all
be warm, be kind, be friendly
and like a kite
sailing in the wind
let this be
your form of travel.

SMOOTH WATERS

I am grateful
that the raging tiger in you
woke up
the sleeping lion in me.

From now on
you won't be placing
your big foot
on my small foot
to squash the life out of me.

I am thankful
you are the one
who pushed me
up and over the wall
to where God is.

Finding myself again
I am no longer
like a lost ship at sea.

With enough tears
drowning the anger
out of me
the waters have become
smooth, clear, and clean.

Every day now
I drink in
the God of my life.

SPIRIT OF TRUTH

Spirit of truth
whizzing around me
like a stinging bee
is not the only irritant
disturbing me.

A spider
spinning her web
till I get tangled in it
can be just as troublesome.

At best
life is a circus
a merry-go-round of sorts
whirling me this way and that.

Growing older
Somebody else comes
with a broomstick in her hand
and sweeps away
the clutter of a lifetime.

Ashamed of the mess I've made,
She gives me a ruler
and says:
Stop measuring your life
by what others think.

Enjoy living
in the fabric of your own skin.

AGING WISELY

Perhaps
we're wearing the ancient garb
of someone who went before us.

Whoever we are
the wrinkled-up woman in us
loves wearing her own rough trod shoes.

Looking into the mirror of our lives
we reminisce
how a sweet, innocent baby
could have burped up the last bit of milk
before it went drooling down
our mother's face.

Beautifully formed then
our innocent lips kissed hers
until blotches of red prettied us up too.

We were small then
and she loved the gurgles in us
as if they were the only song
she wanted to hear.

Today
we are the older wiser ones
wrapping our shabby arms
around our well-worn clothing
and saying to ourselves:
"How good it is to be here."

NO MORE INSOMNIA

My name is Insomnia
and I live
inside the small body
of a girl.

Taking me to bed at night
she dislikes me
for being who I am.

Calls me
the "fret warrior"
when it's herself
muddling over
the messy part of her day.

She loves God immensely
but even God
sometimes appears
like a bandit in her dreams.

Years later
she gets to know
the prickly monster of the night
and tells God
she is it.

From then on
the sleep deprived one
lives, grows and thrives
in being who she is.

DAUGHTER
OF THE EMERALD GREEN ONE

Emerald green
something
beyond lovely
that's the way
you imprinted yourself
upon me.

Taken by surprise
I went about
stammering
your Name.

Even though
I didn't say "God"
I meant God.

Simply put:
That's
what true love
does to you.

You wear it
like a ring.

And among your jewels
it's the only one
you would live
and die for.

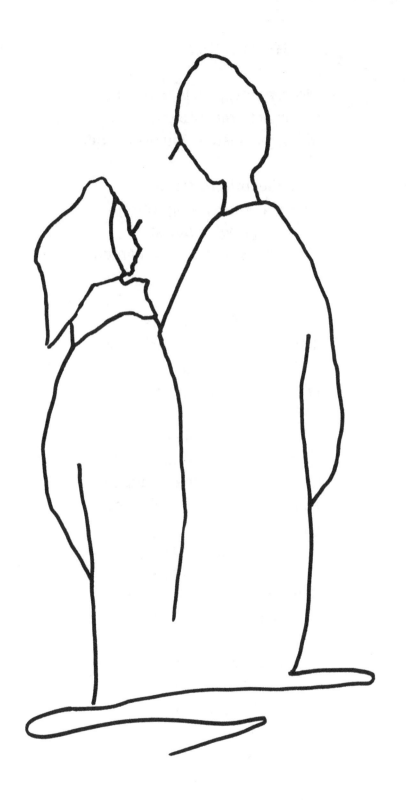

NEW GARDEN OF EDEN

Apricot, apple, peach, plum and pear
you invited me into your orchard
and I began tasting you everywhere.

Beautifully fashioned
I was a young tree
growing quickly
in a soggy part of your garden.

Ripening
before my time
I was the fruit you plucked open
the red apple
whose juicy side had worms in it.

Exposing
the dark side of my nature
I could have been trapped
in the old garden called Eden.

Instead
I chose to have
the sharp fork of a Gardener
go running through me.

And in a moment of pruning
I said to God:
"Wanting goodness
sometimes it takes
being sliced open to get it."

DIVERSITY

Blind girl
wanting to see
accept yourself the way you are
and know
lowly can be lovely.

A child prodigy is a rarity
a gift that makes the world sing
so don't compare yourself
to another.

Born differently
you still
can achieve greatness.

A tiny ant, a small mouse,
a large elephant
they, too,
live on our planet
and the Creator blesses them.

Unique and unrepeatable
each of us is a tiny speck
in our vast universe
neither sitting above
or below another.

We are the orchestra
and diversity
is the song we sing.

GRACEFUL LION

Wild wind
you ripped my jacket open
jumped in and took me by surprise.

Handing me a camera
you said:
"Picture yourself now
and when it gets developed
you will know who you are."

Two days later
a message appeared with the photo:
Sweet, kind, placid on the outside
go down deeper
and meet the roaring lion within.

Older now
I'm learning to tame her
so she doesn't go around
tearing up my skin on the inside
the way others sometimes do.

"Be good to yourself," she says,
"and let the engine in you
travel down a smooth road
not the bumpy one you've been on."

Gracefully
I take her kind paws in mine
and she lies down beside me.

TUNNEL OF LIGHT

When I die
place your hand
on the cemetery of my soul
and rejoice with me
that my hour has come.

Sitting at my funeral ahead of time
I heard this:
A tunnel of light
led you down to the earth
and a tunnel of light will lead you back.

Fearlessly, I left the church
effervescent and joyous
at the thought of it.

Letting all false theologies go
I knew God was not the punisher
some people had erroneously
made Him out to be.

Far from it
He or She was the joyous essence
of the stuff we're all made out of.

With utter contentment
I knew now
there was no better place to be
than going home to the Light
where I came from.

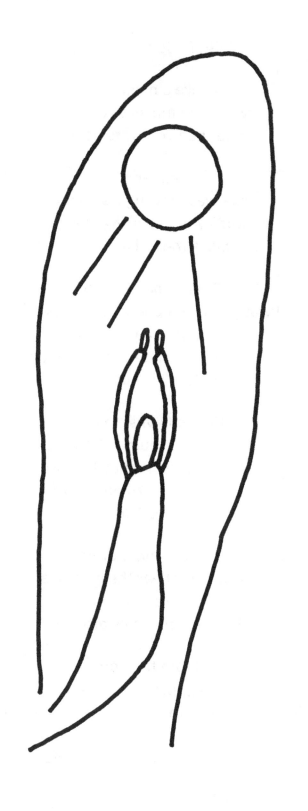

PEACEFUL TRAVELLER

Like a magnet
you drew me into yourself
and then you were gone.

Already
love was growing inside me
and I went spurting along
like a trained athlete.

Out on the highway
I was going at a phenomenal speed
exhilarated and running
on an energy that boosted me up
before I fell down.

Unbeknownst to me
inside the human body
is a mechanism called balance
a switch you turn on and off
to get the rest you need.

Athlete runner or not
if you don't hear the message
a siren
will come screeching after you.

From then on
the great Someone
will be sitting in the driver seat beside you
and together
you will travel the road peacefully.

MELTING THE ICICLE

A stiff face turning chilly on me
I asked myself:
How can love
turn into an ice cube that quickly?

When a friend deserts you that way
it's like stepping into
the cold air of a refrigerator.

Wanting forgiveness
to melt the wall between us
I was young then
too young
for the wall to come down.

Years later
in the warm beat of my heart
something new was percolating.

I can't say for sure what it was
I just know
watering my own icicle
down to nothing
the barrier was gone
finished, forgotten.

No longer living
in a small container
I wrapped my arms
around something big.

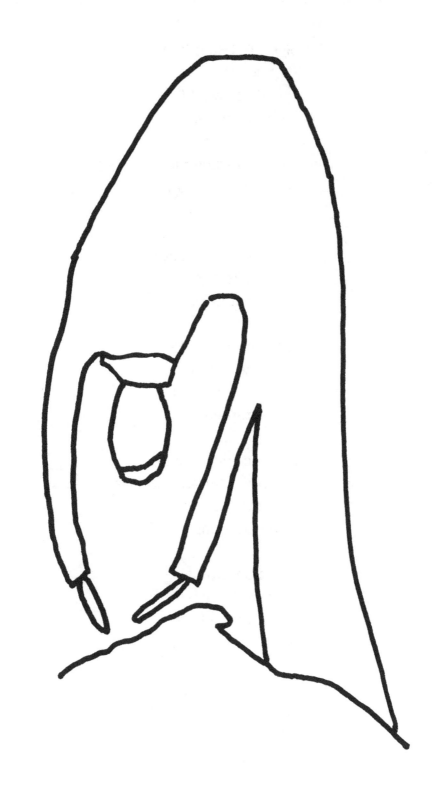

SONG OF THE BELOVED

Dizzy world
hard to be in
I'm looking
for something more
than the doldrums
I've been living in.

Something smooth
like silk
against my skin.

Something elegant
like a robe
I want to wear
forever.

Something close
and intimate
as if the face of God
could be anything but that.

Something
not thwarted
but care-free
and light-hearted.

Something
worth plummeting into
every day of your life.
This is my God.

FIRE OF GOD

A burnt-out candle
on a cold day.

I wish
it was otherwise
but the truth is
I've lost my flame.

The soft wax
I once had
has hardened
in me.

The glow has gone
and in its place
I've seen
what true radiance
looks like.

Touched it
felt it
known it
in the scarred face
of another.

And in the warmth
of my own
true fire
I've said:
"Holy be your Name."

LUMINOUS BEINGS

Harsh words
swift
and cutting:
not the music
I like to hear
but it does purify me
from the inside-out.

Treating me shabbily
if you think a handkerchief
can wipe away my tears
you've got it all wrong.

It's not you
but I
who need to stop
being stationary.

I need to take
a leap forward
up and over the fence
to where new vistas lie.

I need to pop myself open
to stop sheltering
the light
when it wants to come in.

I need to go
where the luminous ones go.

SOUL LIGHT

Too much metal
in my brain
is the negativity holding me down.

What I need
is something positive
a tidal wave of laughter
to lift this darkness from me.

Shifting my energy
I need to stop rolling
backward down a hill
when I am meant
to go forward.

Picking myself up
I need to love
the ridiculous part
of the tragic clown
in me.

The witty
beautiful part
I keep hidden
under a lamp stand.

I need the light
that is in me
to come
shining through.

PURITY WITHIN

Life
can be flowing
like the wind
but not always.

Sometimes
the muck of it
gets filtered in
and like bad breath
you wish it weren't there.

Wrestling
with yourself
it's the smog
on the dark side
of your soul
that must get lifted
the fog that holds you in.

Only then can you say:
"Purity
is the whiteness
of a new moon
rising in me.

So pure am I
not even
an eclipse of the sun
can block out
the new Light pouring in."

LUSCIOUS TREES

Blizzards, snowstorms, sunny days
weather changes daily and so do I.

I'm a seasonal creature
mostly optimistic
injecting joy into a rainy day
and covering up the place
where mud gets in.

On a dull day
you may find me glowing like the sun
but the bad news is
I've hidden from you
the dark mass of nothing energy
I've fallen into.

It's my time to germinate
and when I return
you will see how the green grass
on the dead part of me
has been brought back to life.

No longer hiding my identity
I'll be the greenest
of the green trees.

Standing in the field with you
we'll be gazing
at that
which is luscious in us.

CONTENTMENT

Said the malformed girl:
Did I tell you
there's a flood in my basement
not the kind you would like to see?

It's like picking myself up
the wrong way
and as much as I would like
to flow like a river
dead emotions
have made me stagnant
like a slimy stream.

Scrubbing myself up
sometimes I feel
like a clean pond
and, yet,
there is a dark ditch in me.

I suppose you could say:
It's the black side of my soul
wanting to be washed clean.

Plunging myself downward
I can feel the pure water
from a tap
go dripping through me.

I am at peace now
in the basement of my being.

THE SOUL'S BODY

Berserk
is when the mad bomb
explodes within you.

From now on
cultivate gentleness
but know yourself
fully.

Like a porcupine
some people
carry prickles
in them
and bluntly put
so do you.

Pretending
to be
a soft furry creature
when you're not
is equally damaging.

If you're looking for
the true light
stop camouflaging it.

Your body
is the temple
of your soul
so listen to her.

STURDY MOUSE

Small as a tiny mouse
sitting at the driver's wheel
I don't question
who's in charge of my destiny.

I just put my foot
on the gas pedal knowingly
and go
where the car takes me.

Sometimes
I'm out on the highway
and people bump into me
the wrong way.

They push me over
to the side of the curb
and yell out insanities
reminding me
that I too have my own.

As much as I want
to spit out their words
that get shovelled into me
I hold my tongue still.

I'm a small mouse
strong and sturdy
not to be knocked over
by a giant that stands in my way.

SONG OF THE BAGPIPES

I awoke
to the sound
of bagpipes
playing in me.

Picking up
their melodic tune
I felt the rush of it
flow through.

Without a discordant note
anywhere
it was as if my life
was being pushed forward
on wheels.

I was on a roll now
where even the bumpy road
became smooth.

Inebriated
by my new found joy
if dead cells
could bounce back to life
mine were doing it for me.

If the energy of God
is permanent
this time
I knew it now.

LIFE AFTER DEATH

Pushing aside all fear
I stand beside You
like a thunder cloud
where the rain
comes pouring in.

Love drenches me that way
and I feel
like I could live forever
in the water of it.

Then comes lightening
and I cringe like a bolt
under the blinding brightness
of it.

Removing the scales from my eyes
You plunge me into a landscape
bigger than anything
I've known before.

Just as I've grown
to love it here
You quiet me down to nothing
to the zero point
of my existence.

Reality kisses me on the cheek
and You take my hand in Yours
to wherever we are going.

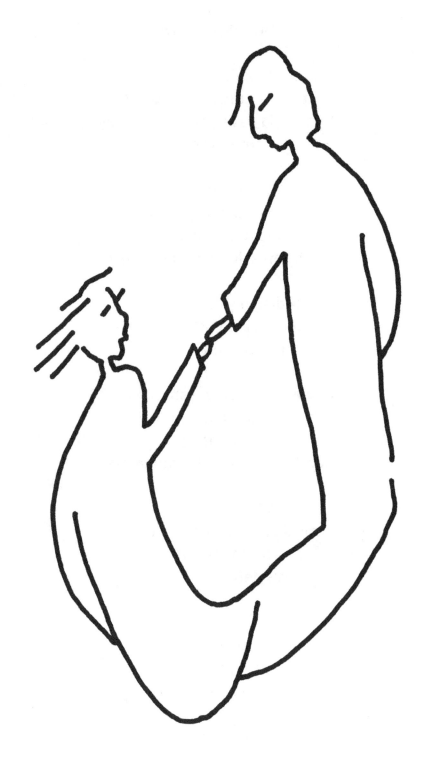

DIVINE MELODY

Like flute music
playing softly in the wind
that could have been my destiny
but it wasn't.

Instead
I came swirling down
into a human body
with soft skin that tears easily.

Hiding my vulnerability
each time life pushed me over
I bounced back up.

With incredible stamina
I kept jumping through
the hoops of life
until the last one flattened me.

Without energy
my dead body got pulled up
by an escalator
that was definitely not human.

Immersed in Divinity
the flawed part of me
came back to life
fully alive
with a new kind of zest
flowing through me.

SELF ACCEPTANCE

Hungering for something deeper
than frothy words
superficiality
was the isolated chair I sat on.

Allowing falsity to hit me
like a bullet
I waited for truth
to come in
and when it did, I rejoiced exceedingly.

This time
even a harsh voice
lost its power
to crumple me.

Perhaps that's all it took
the rough energy of another
to return me home to loving myself.

More authentic now
you won't find me
wearing a plastic face
over the real one.

Instead
you'll find me sitting on my doorstep
saying:
"The frog croaks, the dog barks
the cat mews, the crow caws,"
and everyone's happy just being who they are.

BIRTHING OF THE TRUE SELF

The time for shredding
had come
and like a top
she began unwinding herself
from top to bottom.

Showing up as her true self
she let the world know
she was nobody's toy
to be played with.

Entering a room this way
even the wicked dragon
of fear
coiled its tail
under her.

Shame
hung down its head
and anger
was no more.

Erasing the word ugly
from her vocabulary
she replaced it
with something beautiful.

A new gown
to adorn her
on this the day of her birth.

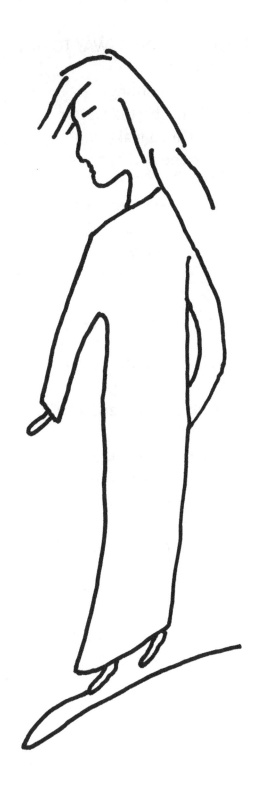

EXPANSIVE BRIDGEWAY TO GOD

Sitting
in uncharted waters
I am a leaky boat
gone adrift at sea.

No one sees me
hears me
knows me
only God.

Reaching out my hand
I say:
"You are the bridge
and I
the clogged water under it."

Yes, comes the Voice,
You are that.
Now choose
something bigger
than puny.

Something free sailing
and smooth
something broad and wide
like the wing of an eagle.

Now cast your eyes upward
and let
the soaring begin.

UNRAVELLING THE PUZZLE

Losing touch
with my own symmetry
I am not the jigsaw
you thought me to be.

Each piece
perfectly assembled
on a table
has left me
in disarray.

Scattered in all directions
the raucous side
of my gypsy mind
can no longer deceive me.

What I need
is a God in motion
something vigorous
like turning the table over.

Standing on it
if need be
and saying:
"When I am alive
fully alive
nothing
not even a shattered puzzle
shall have power
over me."

LIVE LAVISHLY

Locked up
in a dog house of sorts
is the old habitat you lived in.

You followed the rules
and they were good ones
but too narrow
for the adventure that was yours.

It took initiative to tell yourself:
Stop being a shy puppy
but when you did
your bones were full of vigour.

Your tail wagged
and even the hair
on top of your head
stood upright
in the wind.

There was something electric
about you
something brilliant
so brilliant
that even your eyes shone
with the glow of it.

You were a small animal
but the Energy in you
was huge.

PANDEMIC BIRD SONG

I'm a pandemic bird
living in isolation
with myself.

My beak points inward
and I hear
something ethereal
the transcendent music
of another world.

High notes
low notes
exquisite notes
in every chord
of my being.

Something exotic
so exotic
I want to give it
a name
but cannot.

And so
momentarily
I call myself Sublimity
and like a soft cloud
rolling down a hill
I get to touch her
that way.

I AM YOU

Fear Me not:
Wherever you are
I am.

Even when you run
from me
I come toward you.

Push me out of your life
and I will find
a way back in.

Try breathing
without me
and you will see
how stale
the air can be.

If it's oxygen
you need
open your mouth now
and relish it
as never before.

I am the love of your life
and wherever you go
I am.

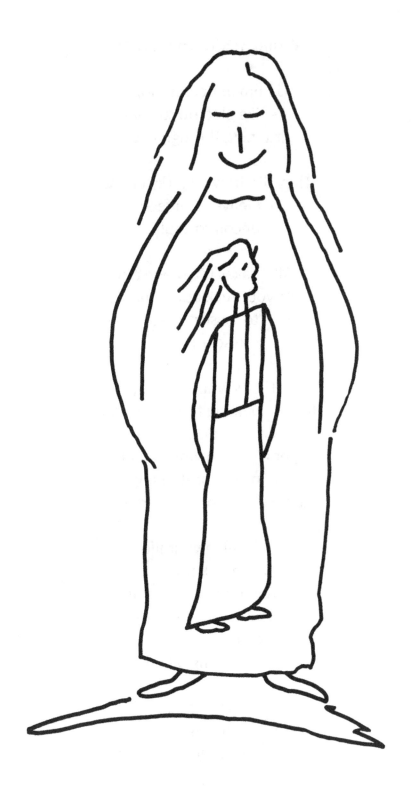

WHIRL YOUR OWN BATON

Jammed up emotions
are like electric currents
running through you.

They discharge a jerky energy
that leaves you feeling
uncomfortable.

All it takes is a down day
for your reckless thoughts
to be scattered
elsewhere.

That's when you say
to the spinning top within you:
Calm yourself down
get a grip on who you are
and stop pretending
to be the acrobat you're not.

Examine your life
and know
that in the circus of it
even a twisted rope
can gear you up
for something beautiful.

In the end
nobody can whirl a baton
the way you can.

TALL ANT

Content
utterly content
I'm a small ant
climbing up
the sleeve of God.

In my ignorance
I have no idea
how I got to be there.

Insignificant as I am
some say:
Keep aspiring
to greatness.
It's the gift
of your birthright.

Stomped on
by the foot of a bully
others see it differently.

Shove you aside
as if they
are the winner.

But you
standing
on the stamina of God
are taller
than they are.

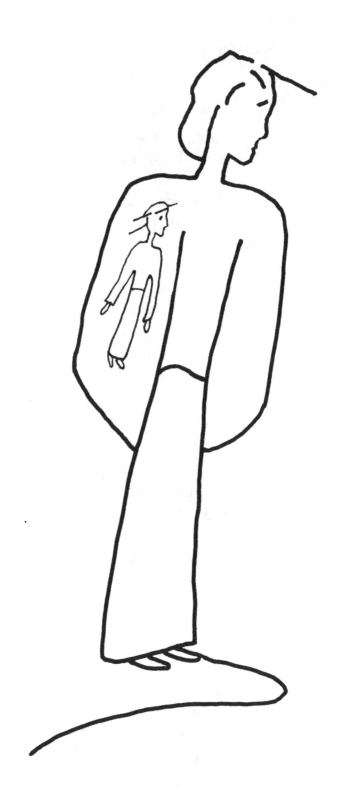

FOOTPRINT OF THE BELOVED
MADE REAL

Footprint of the Beloved:
You, I, others
we're all part of it.

Evolution says:
Beyond Infinity
is where the Beloved goes.

And, yet,
I've seen the Beloved's face
imprinted on your face
my face
everyone's face.

Even the lure
of my soul
tells me:
Lift the veil
and you will see.

Trees, flowers, cats, dogs
everything
has the footprint of the Beloved
on it.

It's in our DNA
so why distance ourselves
when the touch of Love
is as near to me
as it is to you?

WOMEN OF LIGHT

Picture this:
dark eyes
tears large enough
to fill an ocean liner gone astray.

Insipid and emotionally dry
it's the lost woman
the estranged one
in you and others
drumming up love
when there is none.

Sailing in a small ship
turned overboard
you cannot honour
someone else's grief
when it is your own.

Neither
can you master the waves
until you plunge into them.

Brave soul
take hold
of the reins of your life.

Let in
the Light of this new day
and hide not
your scarred skin from it.

PURIFICATION OF A GYPSY SOUL

Ripped open, torn apart
that's what it took
to awaken the quiet soul
of this whirling gypsy.

No one suspected
the danger she was in
least of all the gypsy
who tripped over life
as if her blind eyes could see.

Taken by surprise
it was a revolutionary journey
she was on
and nothing
short of an explosion
could awaken her now.

Whirled inward
what she wanted she got:
a tornado of dark energy
that was not someone else's
but her own.

Digesting it
was never easy.

And, yet,
opening the latch of her soul
she found something immaculate in it.

MELLOW ME DOWN

Sometimes
all it takes
is a thorn in the chest
to make you more real.

Get to know me this way
and you will see
I am a small creature
whose soft nails
have claws within them.

Sitting quietly in my raging mind
the animal in me
tells me not to pounce on anyone.

Feeling the fangs in my own teeth
I must not use them
to harm myself or anyone
in disagreement with me.

I must aspire to the higher Energy
knowing
that each time I get pushed backward
there is a God who propels me forward.

Who says:
Only my kind of Love
can soften the tough skin
around the cement wall
that has grown hard within you.

MOUTHPIECE OF GOD

You could say
Infinity is the gold ink
flowing through
Someone else's pen into yours.

That being the case,
I said to God:
"I am the wide-open book
ready to be written on."

Premature, came the response.
You're not ready for anything
until the calmness of a still lake
flows through you.

Accustomed to harshness from others
but not from God
I got tangled
in the river waters of my own debris.

In the waiting time I sometimes felt
like a baby in an incubator
waiting to give birth to
I know not what.

Finally
the day came.
Infinity handed me her pen
and said:
Become the mouthpiece of God!

BIRTHING OF A WHITE OWL

As with all eggs
in the beginning,
I shrank down to nothing
and became everything
in the One who made me big.

Throbbing with joy
I could feel the birthing
of a new being within me.

Who
and what would I be
when my half-formed wings
were flapping under me?

Already
I was being formed
and shaped
into something beautiful.

My yellow eyes
carried a strange wisdom in them
far beyond
the birthing of my years.

Preening my feathers
the universal One
named me White Owl
and I flew out of her hands
for all to see.

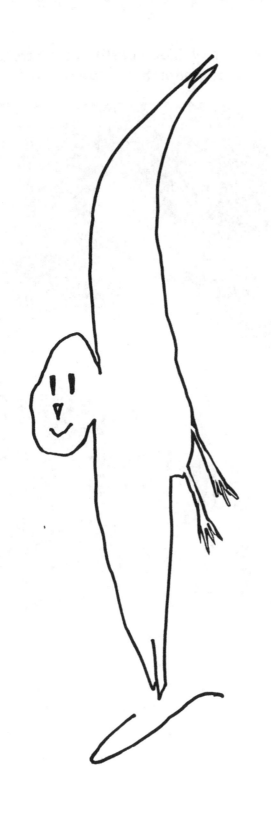

Picture of Eileen Curteis in the trees
Photo and art piece: Carey Pallister

"The deeper the roots of a tree
penetrate the earth
the greater the chance it has
to grow, rise into the air
and produce fruit."
- Blessed Marie Anne Blondin

ABOUT THE AUTHOR

For the last 30 years, Eileen Curteis, a Sister of Saint Anne has been involved in the Reiki Healing Ministry, a revered eastern healing art that she combines with her Christian heritage of healing. A former teacher, principal and educator for 27 years, Eileen shares that her greatest passion now lies in her healing ministry and in the literary arts. She has authored fourteen books to date and has become an accomplished poet, artist and writer, as well as being a producer of seven CDs and three films. She lives in Victoria, BC.

You can view Eileen's other books on Amazon, Barnes and Noble and other book retailers worldwide.

CPSIA information can be obtained
at www.ICGtesting.com
Printed in the USA
BVHW030737090922
646520BV00008B/174